The Future of Careers

The Chartered Institute of Personnel and Development is the leading publisher of books and reports for personnel and training professionals, students, and all those concerned with the effective management and development of people at work. For full details of all our titles, please contact the Publishing Department:

Tel: 020 8263 3387
Fax: 020 8263 3850

E-mail: publish@cipd.co.uk

The catalogue of all CIPD titles can be viewed on the CIPD website:
www.cipd.co.uk/publications

The Future of Careers

Richard Donkin
Helen Wilkinson
Bruce Tulgan
Ralph Tribe
John Mockler
Wendy Hirsh

First published 2002

Cover design by Curve
Designed and typeset by Beacon GDT
Printed in Great Britain by the Short Run Press, Exeter

British Library Cataloguing in Publication Data
A catalogue record for this book is available from the British Library

ISBN 0 85292 965 X

Chartered Institute of Personnel and Development,
CIPD House, Camp Road, London SW19 4UX

Tel: 020 8971 9000
Fax: 020 8263 3333
Website: www.cipd.co.uk

Incorporated by Royal Charter. Registered charity no. 1079797.

Contents

Acknowledgement

The CIPD would like to thank Phillip Hadridge for leading the contributor workshop in March 2002.

Foreword

No matter what stage of their career they are at, most people are no longer completely certain about what their future career path will look like. Even the word 'career' can sound inadequate to describe the non-linear (and often confusing or accidental) routes that people take – from permanent contract to self-employment, to career break, and back again – sometimes in parallel.

The old rules no longer seem to apply, but the much anticipated new world of work has not been fully realised either. There are gaps between individuals and organisations which don't allow for honest conversations about careers. Career management is seen as a 'treat' for the chosen few, offered when employees are leaving their employers through redundancy, or dealt with once a year in an appraisal. Different groups of people are taking on new career patterns and organisations need to respond. The strong business argument that to develop a dialogue with all employees about their careers should help them – and the business – to achieve their full potential is not acknowledged or, if it is, there is a lot of uncertainty about how to do it.

It is not easy to get career management right, but it is essential for the future – not just of careers but for individuals and business itself.

The Future of Careers is the latest in several scenarios-based futures publications commissioned by the CIPD. These include *The Future of Learning for Work* and *The Future of Reward*.

All three explore what could happen to work in the future, and who will have to take action to make those scenarios a reality.

In *The Future of Careers*, six leading commentators on HR and careers were invited to give their view of how the future of careers might look and of what issues will be most important in promoting these changes. The contributions focus variously on the role of the individual, organisation and government in shaping new ways of building the career. We hope that the final result is a combination of views and ideas that will stimulate the debate on what a career means, and how it should be managed and developed for the benefit of organisations, communities and individuals.

Imogen Daniels
Adviser, Development and Resourcing
Chartered Institute of Personnel and Development

Jennifer Schramm
Adviser, Training and Development
Chartered Institute of Personnel and Development

Executive summary

Chapter 1
Fusing the career with the lifestyle
Richard Donkin

Journalist and author of *Blood, Sweat and Tears: The evolution of work*, Richard Donkin looks at scenarios for career development in a world where the concept of career has fused more closely with that of lifestyle, and where the government takes an active role in promoting entrepreneurialism.

Chapter 2
The future of careers in a mobile work culture
Helen Wilkinson

Helen Wilkinson, founder of genderquake.com, focuses on a future in which 'mosaic careers in a DIY economy' means that organisations are increasingly reliant on the self-employed, freelancers, consultants and entrepreneurs. These workers neither have nor want a traditional career path inside an organisation. What do organisations have to do to develop more constructive relationships with this new breed of workers, and how should they respond to the looser career structures now evolving?

Chapter 3
Creating the customised career
Bruce Tulgan

Founder of RainmakerThinking and author of *Winning the Talent War* and *Managing Generation X*, Bruce Tulgan explores how shifting generations in the workforce and the war for talent could bring about a world of work in which the customised dream job is no longer a dream.

Chapter 4
The self-managed career – the key to the future can be found in the past
Ralph Tribe

Ralph Tribe, Vice-president Human Resources at Getty Images, looks at how the self-managed career resembles work patterns of the past and holds the key to future success. To participate in that success the organisation of the future will have to be able to offer the type of work that transforms a 'jobber' into a 'careerist' or otherwise risk alienating a large proportion of its workforce.

Chapter 5
*Careers don't stop at 50 – where are the people
for the future?*
John Mockler

Head of Human Resources, Tate, John Mockler
looks at the necessary inclusion and development
of older workers in future career patterns.
Exploring their value to organisations in meeting
skills shortages and boosting knowledge-sharing
and career development through coaching roles,
John argues that older workers will be increasingly
important in the future.

Chapter 6
Careers in organisations – time to get positive
Wendy Hirsh

Wendy Hirsh, independent researcher and
consultant and co-author of *Planning Your Own
Career*, examines how organisations need to
rethink what is meant by the career, why careers
matter to both individuals and organisations, and
how career development really takes place and
who is responsible for making it happen.

Richard Donkin is an international author, speaker and commentator on management and employment issues. His first book, *Blood Sweat and Tears: The evolution of work*, was warmly received and extensively reviewed in the UK and the USA.

For the past eight years he has been recruitment columnist for the *Financial Times*, a position he now fills in a freelance capacity after leaving the full-time staff of the FT in January 2002. He established and edited FT CareerPoint.com, a Financial Times Internet service, aimed at delivering recruitment services online.

1 | Fusing the career with the lifestyle

Richard Donkin

Past, present and future overlap

Futurism can rarely divorce itself from contemporary fashion. Recall, if you can, the cinema, television and magazine impressions of the future seen through the eyes of the pop art visionaries of the 'swinging 60s'. The 21st century was envisioned as a time of space travel, anti-gravity machines, food in tablet form, Perspex bubbles for housing, and unisex suits made from Crimplene. The future was Tracy Island in *Thunderbirds*.

In later decades, when the fashion for plastics and synthetic fibres had made way once more for natural products, futurists began to foresee nuclear-ravaged landscapes and subsistence scrap-metal societies in perpetual tribal conflict. Invariably, the future is depicted as something quite different from the present. Yet so much social change is shaded by subtlety and nuance. It is impossible, for example, to name the day that it became no longer acceptable in the workplace to call a young woman a 'girl'.

In the same way, we have only the vaguest recollection of the time that large companies began to hand out security passes to enter the building, or the day that voice-mail became available, or the occasion when we sent our first e-mail. But for most of us these three apparently inconsequential yet, with hindsight, significant events would have occurred in the past 10 years.

Who would have thought, back in the 1960s, that knowledge of the QWERTY keyboard – that mainstay of the typing pool – would prove invaluable 40 years on to almost every employee who worked for any part of their day in front of a screen? In this case something from our career past has become a significant feature of our workplace future.

'There is a tendency to assume a greater degree of change than that delivered in reality. Much of the change we experience is gentle, subliminal, graduated and conservative'

Our impressions of the future are influenced deeply by contemporary fashion and mores. There is a tendency also to assume a greater degree of change than that delivered in reality, and to portray change in the way it influences physical appearance rather than attitudes. Much of the change we experience is gentle, subliminal, graduated and conservative. It tends to be restrained by the human love of tradition and nostalgia. I call this phenomenon 'social drag'. Witness the enduring presence of the suit and tie in the office. Whatever happened to dress-down Fridays?

Big, sudden, occasionally cataclysmic change is difficult to foresee. Who, for example, would have predicted the AIDS epidemic of the 1980s – and who, when it happened, would have expected the danger to have been largely forgotten within a generation? Who would have thought that a tiny white pill, allowing women to protect themselves from the risk of conception, would have created a new force in the workplace – career-focused women, delaying their families into their 30s?

Who would have thought then that wide-bodied jets and cheaper air travel would shrink the world into what Marshall McLuhan had described prophetically as 'a global village'? And who would have taken that thinking some way further to predict the re-emergence of homespun values as people became tired of travelling?

These are issues we must confront in any crystal-ball-gazing exercise. We must look at the discernible trends and use them to shape our predictions – but at the same time we must be aware that unforeseen events will send our future path in unexpected directions.

Probable possibilities

So what can we be fairly sure about?

I think we can be certain that the demographic trend towards smaller families will lead to thinning populations in much of the industrialised world. Its impact on employment would suggest that immigration from the current Third World into Europe is going to become an important political and economic issue within the next 20 to 40 years. A smaller, younger population is going to be supporting a large grey bulge of older people. What price retirement in that society?

At the same time medical advances are going to increase the potential for people to live longer. Paradoxically, the prospect will begin to lose its allure. The Dutch have legalised euthanasia. How many other state legislatures will follow suit – and, if and when they do, how will that influence our career and life planning?

How many of the 1990s trends towards more flexible, part-time and contract employment will continue? Will teleworking and homeworking increase? Or will some of these trends fizzle away as technologically inspired fads? How many of these fashions will develop into lifestyles and movements and ideologies, accelerated perhaps by events. We know now that there are large disaffected sections of society prepared and capable of wreaking destruction on the symbols of Western capitalism. How long will it be before the first 'dirty bomb' explodes its radioactive payload over one of our cities? How long before a deadly virus or bacterial plague is released deliberately into the environment? How shall we feel about homeworking when that happens?

We should recognise that many advances in our past have occurred simply because a technology has been created to make them possible. As soon as the materials and techniques were developed to construct tall buildings, the buildings happened. Bridge-building followed suit, but tunnelling had to wait a while longer until capitalism had created sufficient wealth to invest in the connections that could physically link continents.

Let us assume that in the world of 2020 we have become much more closely linked. Broadband has finally provided instant skill-free remote connections for text, video and the spoken word; air travel has become ubiquitous and even cheaper, relatively, than it is today; anyone with a reasonable degree of fitness can climb Everest and survive in protective suits equipped with an oxygen-rich heat-controlled atmosphere. Discovery and travel are no longer characterised by geographical exclusivity but by financial or knowledge- or skill-based exclusivity.

> *'What really matters is access – access to influence, access to quality leisure, access to your family. What you crave is belonging. What you value most are your networks'*

Who you know still matters – but what you know matters more. What you are earning is losing its meaning. What really matters is access – access to influence, access to quality leisure, access to your family. What you crave is belonging. What you value most are your networks linking you to those worlds that define your personal history: the community where you grew up, your old school friends, college and university, clubs, associations, sporting ties, professional associations. Your identity relies not only on your professional skills but on the potential and inclusiveness created by your interlinked histories. Your outlook has to be more than Janus-faced – it has to be multi-faceted, directed intermittently at every point of your personal compass.

It is these connections that furnish you with the means to thrive and develop. You are connected by your investments to the profit centres that are still described as companies. You are connected via agencies and professional networks to your sources of financial income. Your memberships and subscriptions link you to sources of leisure and learning. And your payments to professional web-based service organisations ensure that your domestic affairs are properly administered.

Bad news and good news

Here is the bad news. Not everyone is so fortunate. The levels of service you can command and the size of your network depends to a great extent on your value to society and how you place yourself in your society. You are your brand and your brand must be managed and marketed. You may do some of this yourself, but you might pay for part of the work. Paying to acquire skills, paying to work if those skills can best be acquired on the job, is no longer unusual. This was already happening in the 1990s. If you wanted to be an ocean sailor at that time, you could sign up to an event such as Chay Blyth's global challenge, a round-the-world yacht race. For £20,000 at the prices of the mid- to late 1990s you could acquaint yourself with all the skills needed to crew and, if you studied hard enough, maybe skipper an ocean-going yacht.

The good news is that in 2020, governments have woken up to the new demands of the individual in the workplace. They have introduced legislation to help people maintain their independence as professionals and artisans. Outmoded definitions of what constitutes a worker have been scrapped. What matters most now is getting work done rather than the specific status of those who are employed in work. Tools – computers, telephones, desks and other professional equipment – are becoming more readily available in serviced professional spaces in airports, railway stations, hotels, pubs, cafés, motorway service stations and in various forms of transport.

The infrastructure of free agency is under construction. Education has broadened its focus beyond our early years. Universities, learning centres and teachers are everywhere, and they are accessible. There is a new emphasis on choice. Governments still intervene to ensure that all children are supplied with the basic skills of numeracy and communication. Children still learn to read, write and communicate. But a large part of the curriculum can now be determined by choice. Children are no longer banded into age ranges but ability ranges. A 7-year-old may study French with a 16-year-old and an 11-year-old if they have matching levels of ability. They may take a variety of exams to measure their abilities. They are able to customise a proportion of their learning and education to a greater degree.

The 1990s' obsession with knowledge has been tempered somewhat by a recognition of artisan, entrepreneurial and presentational skills. Children can devote more time, if they wish, to learning trades such as carpentry, plumbing and stonemasonry. There are opportunities at school to earn money, or the more tax-efficient vocational or learning credits, by selling their wares or services in school enterprises. Age barriers at the earlier and later stages of careers have begun to disappear. Long-term guild-based craft apprenticeships have been re-established as standard-bearers of quality. Some of these were introduced by trade unions concerned to be involved in the elevation and marketing of the skills of their members.

The MBA has become institutionalised across the Western world as the ideal qualification for project managers, often heavily supported by venture capital. And the GMAT exam has become a recognised international educational qualification. Some business providers (terms such as 'employers' and 'employees' are still used but only among the rump of large manufacturers, service providers and public sector organisations whose roots remain in the industrial age) have begun to ask to see the GMAT scores and other test certificates of the contractors who work for them. Personality testing has become nationally accredited and the results are included on updateable identity cards that carry a DNA sample of the bearer.

All individuals, even children, are encouraged to have their own limited company. Within another 20 years these personal enterprises will have become formalised in law. Every individual is designated copyright and Internet rights at birth. Each new baby is issued with a birth certificate and personal website.

Our income and outgoings are tracked electronically through our personal companies and taxed accordingly. Governments have begun to study the implications of introducing a cashless society, but any such proposal can expect to be resisted and undermined by those who seek to avoid paying tax. The black economy is reorganising itself on the lines of barter clubs and transactions based on surviving foreign currencies.

Tax thresholds will be raised, however, to allow much higher levels of earnings before the imposition of income tax.

Teaching skills have become more important than ever, and they are combined in some cases with talent-spotting and coaching. Teachers stay close to certain pupils, often on a retained basis, long after formal schooling has ended. Some of these former pupils were academic stars and some were disadvantaged children. Professional and ethical values have not disappeared. Not all professional relationships are determined by an ability to pay. But the transactional basis of workplace relationships has become more transparent.

An increase in individual entrepreneurialism and the sole-trader mentality is putting pressure on the old concept of voluntarism as people begin to attach a price to more and more of their activities. The new concept of voluntarism is founded in opportunity management, justified by its potential for learning and self-promotion.

> *'The old career suggested continuity and vocation. The new career, in some cases, is of limited duration.'*

The concept of the career has fused more closely with that of lifestyle. People rarely use the word 'career' any more, and when they do it is no longer in the singular context in which it was used in the twentieth century. You have parallel careers, careers that interlink, careers that end, and new careers that start mid-way through your lifetime.

The old career suggested continuity and vocation. The new career, in some cases, is of limited duration.

In these circumstances people have grown as uncertain of a career as they are of marriage, delaying their entry into a vocation or profession until they feel sure they have found something they really want to do. Even then they keep their options open. University careers services have become redundant, replaced by web-based information and contract-offering centres that can reflect the ever-growing variety of work emerging in the Internet age.

So what does the career look like in this world?

For some people it has not changed too radically. The legal profession has succeeded in protecting its privileges. People are still called to the bar. But many professions have been internationalised. An accountant, a pharmacist and a general practitioner can work anywhere in the world since their qualifications have been standardised internationally.

Careers in information and communications technology have become piecemeal and project-based, involving periods of paid work interwoven with new learning and technology updates. Specialists have become more sought after than generalists, and general managers have all but disappeared at the highest levels. Management is

no longer a specialist skill but a skill taught to everyone. People management has become the management of transactions and relationships between customers and suppliers. The budget-holding customer manager is highly visible in what remains of every employing organisation.

European employment laws have reached a uniformity of a sort, tiers of regulations reflecting regional differences. The European Commission has been persuaded, finally, that flexibility is not the enemy of the job and that full-time permanent employment is no longer the holy grail of the European worker.

Every European citizen is equipped with an employment account that keeps a running total of pension entitlements, projects undertaken and taxes paid. Many more people have become sole traders, finding work through agencies. The agency brand has become the employee brand in many careers. In manufacturing, annualised hours contracts and sector pay agreements have replaced standard working weeks. In this way, the French-led 35-hour week has proved a success – and it is now beginning to influence working practices in Japan and the USA.

The search for cheap labour has changed radically as companies respond to consumer- and investor-led demands to outlaw unacceptable working practices among suppliers. The Nike code has become the manufacturing industry standard the world over.

One unexpected outcome of an ageing society is a return to family values. The fragmentation of society is in reverse. The new middle classes are having more children and looking after their elderly, often dependent, parents. The increased success of women in the workplace has won improved maternity and childcare rights. Career breaks have become acceptable, underpinned by legislation and supported by career re-entry courses. This has had the knock-on effect of renewing women's maternal instincts, particularly among those who regret the remoteness of their upbringing by older mothers who spent much of their time at work.

On the downside, people are still struggling to match their earnings aspirations with their desired lifestyle. At least these days they are less worried about the career ladder, since that has all but disappeared. Promotion is about selling your personal brand rather than moving up a hierarchy. Bosses have become an endangered species. Today the people who used to be bosses are customers who reward you for whatever skill or service you can provide. They can't promote you because their relationship with a profit centre is also contractual. All of you are part of a project-based team. Some of the people you work alongside have worked with you before, and you relate to each other not through lines of authority but through lines of mutual respect. That is the way a career works now.

Helen Wilkinson is a regular commentator on the changing world of work. She is the founder-director of Genderquake Limited, a strategic consultancy focused on the gender dynamics of social, economic and technological change (www.genderquake.com). She is also the founder of www.elancentric.com, the first business community for elancers and elancentric networks, associations and organisations in the UK. A pioneering member of the think-tank Demos, she now sits on its Advisory Council.

2 | The future of careers in a mobile work culture

Helen Wilkinson

What does the future hold for careers and professional development in an increasingly mobile work culture?

The question is an important one – both for individuals and for organisations and for the economy as a whole. After all, career structures have been the principal vehicle through which commitment is engaged and re-engaged over time – and a means of recruiting and retaining talented staff. The dissolution of traditional career structures, and the lack of clarity about what replaces them, is likely to have an impact on future economic success.

This chapter begins by depicting one possible scenario for careers in the year 2050 – the 'anti-careers scenario'. It is a story of disconnection, of a breakdown in communication and trust between the new generation of workers and large organisations, and of a retreat from the very idea of careers.

The remainder of the chapter works backwards from this opening scenario in order to investigate how we can prevent it from becoming tomorrow's future through the actions we take today.

2050 – a world of anti-careers

By 2050 knowledge-based industries will be the norm. Fundamental shifts already occurring in our social and economic landscape will have produced seismic changes in the world of work. According to the Institute for Employment Studies, 'knowledge work' is forecast to increase its share of work distribution from 37 per cent in 1996 to 40 per cent in 2006. By 2050 knowledge-based industries will define the economy. But knowledge will no longer be deposited in large organisations. It will be dispersed and fragmented.

The growth sectors of the economy are not the large 'employing' organisations but small businesses, self-employment, and what Thomas Malone – professor of information services at the MIT School of Management – has dubbed 'the elance economy', an economy which relies on outsourcing, subcontracting and remote management, and in which free agents move flexibly from project to project.

'The economy will be divided into two parallel business cultures – the culture of large-scale organisations alongside a DIY culture.'

Knowledge capital will increasingly be mobile, and the knowledge clusters of the economy will be highly fragmented and individualised. The economy will have singularly failed to transmit knowledge in organisations systemically, not least because one of the principal vehicles for doing so – the career – will be increasingly redundant as a concept for engaging employee commitment or attracting new workers into large organisations.

The dominant work culture will be distrustful and anti-careerist, and individuals no longer have the confidence to look to government and/or large-scale organisations to take care of their career and training needs. If individuals once aspired to be working in a large organisation with a career for life, in 2050 they now aspire to be a member of the DIY economy – living off their wits and know-how, and dependent on themselves.

Employers and large organisations will have lost out in the war for talent and will be continually struggling to recruit and retain the brightest and the best.

The most creative and intelligent brains will be working in the DIY economy of elancers, entrepreneurs and free agents. And through necessity as much as free will, large organisations and 'employing' organisations will increasingly be dependent on these freelance workers, consultants and small and medium-sized enterprises (SMEs) for core knowledge-based activities.

Partly because of this, the economy will be divided into two parallel business cultures – the culture of large-scale organisations where employee morale, commitment and trust is low, alongside a DIY culture of the highly skilled and valued self-employed, freelancers, elancers, consultants, entrepreneurs and workers in SMEs who supply services and ideas to the mainstream economy.

This scenario is a direct result of the failure of large-scale employers and organisations to harness the knowledge, creativity and innovation of the new generation of workers and to embrace and assimilate their values, their working styles and approaches within the mainstream organisational culture and economy.

By 2050 the outsourcing of knowledge work will be inherently problematic, leaving large organisations vulnerable to competition, and perhaps more importantly, to knowledge transfer in what will be a highly competitive, as opposed to collaborative, knowledge-based economy.

Large-scale organisations will be less able to control and police their intellectual property because their knowledge capital will increasingly be dependent on these looser elance arrangements. Tough contracts will be ineffective as sanctions since the costs of policing and enforcing them will be so high, and the real damage from knowledge transfer will have taken place.

The failure to build a new psychological contract with the new breed of independent-minded worker will be a problem in other ways. These free workers will tend to view employers and large organisations in self-interested terms, lacking loyalty and commitment, and having no compunction about working for a rival firm the next day. The belated attempt of some organisations to attract and retain these workers by offering revamped career structures will not work because belief and trust in the idea of organisational career structures will have long gone.

After 50 years of organisational retreat from responsibility for managing career structures and professional development, learning will be done 'on the job' and at the large organisation's expense. The mistakes from on-the-job learning will not build knowledge, expertise and know-how in-house because organisations will be dependent on freelance workers and smaller firms. Knowledge will consistently be 'leaking' out of organisations.

The workers who remain employees of large organisations will also be resentful, distrustful and envious of the free workers in the DIY economy. For them, as with the free workers, the belated attempt to secure loyalty and commitment through the promise of revamped career structures will fall on deaf ears.

Partly because of this, the knowledge ecology of large organisations – far from delivering creativity, innovation, and collaboration – will be fragmented and ultimately uncompetitive. Britain will be in danger of losing out to other countries that have taken collective responsibility for careers and professional development.

Where we are today

It's a pessimistic scenario – but the seeds of that future are being sown today. If organisations continue to abdicate responsibility, there are good grounds for believing that the scenario outlined above will become tomorrow's reality.

Survey after survey reports that trust between employers and employees is low, and that workers feel let down by large organisations. Attitudes to self-employment and entrepreneurialism are more positive.

But it doesn't have to be like this. The seeds of an alternative future are also being sown in the present. We must nurture these if we are to avoid the scenario described above.

Organisational retreat

Organisations have been in retreat from the hierarchical linear career for almost two decades. The reasons are not hard to comprehend.

Fundamental restructuring of the economy began in the late 1970s and accelerated in the 1980s and 1990s. The shift from manufacturing to services ushered in a more insecure age for workers. At the lower income levels and in the manufacturing sector, apprenticeships fell away. At the professional level, the downsizing and de-layering of organisations in the 1980s symbolised a new era and represented the end of the psychologically comfortable jobs-for-life concept.

As management layers were stripped away in large organisations, swathes of middle managers lost their jobs, experiencing unemployment and insecurity for the first time in their lives. Faith in the linear hierarchical career structure was shaken to the core, and trust and confidence between employer and employee was lost. A new generation – Generation X – who entered the labour market at this time internalised the lessons. They were going to rely only on themselves.

Writers and gurus consistently talk about the need to re-engage employee commitment, not with old-style career structures and promises but with new kinds of employee benefits (work–life benefits, flexible working, and the like) and a new psychological contract. If organisations can no longer offer people careers for life, so the argument has gone, they can at least promise them a high quality of working life while they work for them.

The decline of organisational hierarchies and the erosion of the linear career model also brought a new concept of careers into focus. Individuals, rather than employers, we are told, must assume responsibility for their careers – building up a portfolio of skills from job to job, project to project, in a new career mosaic.

Although some workers – younger rather than older, and women rather than men – may feel more at ease with this approach, partly because they had less vested in the old career structures, the vast majority have been uneasy with organisational retreat from careers.

The de-institutionalisation of work

The unease that many people feel reflects a deeper anxiety about the way work is being stripped of its institutional meaning.

Employment is a major vehicle for socialisation, offering people ready-made structures, timetables and routines, as well as a community. Our culture has institutionalised learning and work for almost 200 years, so it is hardly surprising that individuals are uneasy with the sudden removal of this institutional framework. The freedom and autonomy that accompanies self-employment and entrepreneurship may be appealing to a growing minority, but in practice the vast majority of workers would prefer a more structured work environment.

In the industrial and modern eras, people traded freedom and autonomy for security and stability. Working lives were institutionalised through organisations and their hierarchies – as employer and employee – and were developed and sustained over time through career frameworks. Loyalty and commitment were rewarded with progression up the career ladder.

The shift to post-industrial society – the decline of manufacturing, the erosion of large-scale organisations and the downsizing that took place in the 1980s – put some of these trends into reverse and began a period in which work and careers were partly de-institutionalised. Apprenticeships became a thing of the past. Career structures began to lose their meaning. Workers began to assimilate the message that careers and their livelihood were now their individual responsibility rather than the responsibility of the employer or of society as a whole.

In important ways, the de-institutionalisation of work and career structures remains the dominant concept still today. The idea of the structured linear career has been replaced by the idea of the mosaic non-hierarchical portfolio career in which people move around from job to job, and from project to project, garnering transferable skills as they go. But the idea that they might look to an employer or to a large-scale organisation to be responsible for their career and training needs is considered increasingly irrelevant – or wishful thinking.

A new generation of workers

The rhetoric of individualisation, de-institutionalisation and the anti-career ethos has been most easily encapsulated and understood in research and writing about Generation X – that breed of workers (the eldest of whom are now in their 30s) who witnessed the de-institutionalisation of careers and the retreat from collective responsibility at a formative stage in their professional development. It is that generation which is seen not just to embody the anti-career ethos – remember Ben Stiller's 1994 film *Reality Bites* or Douglas Coupland's book *Generation X*? – but to be most at ease with project-based work and with taking personal responsibility for their own professional development.

> *'The de-institutionalisation of work and career structures remains the dominant concept still today. The idea of the structured linear career has been replaced by the idea of the mosaic non-hierarchical portfolio career.'*

These workers are certainly more comfortable with self-employment and exhibit more entrepreneurial attitudes. Their individualism is reinforced by a deep-seated distrust of the commitment of employers and large-scale organisations to meet their needs, and of the capacity and willingness of the government to tackle the issues.

Organisations have failed to harness their values and working styles and bring them into the lifeblood of organisational cultures.

The feminisation of work

The feminisation of work has been another striking trend. Women's entry into the workforce has posed new challenges to organisational cultures and workplace values – challenges to which many large organisations together with the mainstream economy have found it difficult to respond.

The mainstream work culture has been slow to adapt – and since the mid-1990s there have been reports of women opting out of large-scale organisations to set up on their own. Self-employment rates and rates of setting up in business among women have increased significantly during this period. A DIY 'genderquake' economy is forming, which engages with, but appears unable to transform, the mainstream economy.

The DIY economy

All these trends have been the catalyst for the birth of a new breed of worker: the self-employed, the consultant, the small businessperson, the man or woman who opts out of traditional career structures in large organisations. They are the people who have rejected the traditional career route and struck out on their own.

This new breed of workers is creating cultural challenges for large organisations. They are promoting new ways of working, and are living the new 'career mosaic'. They are also garnering new recruits, by default as much as by design.

The crisis of confidence and faith that many workers are experiencing with large-scale employers is accelerating the trends towards self-employment, freelancing, entrepreneurialism and project work. There is also growing awareness that fundamental structural shifts in the nature of work mean that people will have several work transitions over the course of the life-cycle. Working in the DIY economy – in self-employment, consultancy, and elancing – is likely to become part of this, whether by choice or by happenstance.

Many 40-something baby-boomers who fell victim to organisational restructuring and downsizing in the late 1980s and 1990s came to rely on this way of working – as interim executives and consultants. In the process they discovered new freedoms: power without responsibility, and a less stressful way of life. For Generation X – the 20- and 30-somethings – self-reliance through self-employment, entrepreneurship and elancing has often seemed more desirable than selling their souls to large organisations. It has also represented the means of creating some semblance of security in a risky and volatile world of work.

Worker guilds and mutuals

These independent-minded workers are having to take responsibility because others – organisations and the government – have largely abdicated theirs. Yet although they have learned the hard way that they must rely on themselves, they are also at the forefront of creating new networks, associations and organisational forms within which they can begin to construct narratives about their working lives, the pathways they are forging and the career mosaics they are putting together. They have learned that they should collaborate with other like-minded people to make sense of their working lives and plan for the future.

Through the 1980s and 1990s, work-based networks and associations began to proliferate, whether for women, for freelancers or for specific professionals and artisans. These intermediate networks and associations have become forums for peer-based learning – knowledge exchange, skills transfer, peer-to-peer support, informal learning and professional development. Both informal and formal, they are filling the gap that organisations and the government have failed to fill.

In some ways their emergence reflects the culture gap that exists between changing values and lifestyle experiences and the supporting infrastructure offered by organisations. They have their parallels both in the trade guilds of the pre-industrial era, and in the guilds, professional associations and unions that emerged with the advent of the last industrial revolution to represent and champion the lifestyle of the industrial worker.

The re-institutionalisation of work

These trends suggest that a new and important shift is under way.

We are on the edge of experiencing a 're-institutionalisation' of work. The clock has not gone back all the way, and collective action is taking a very different form, but a process of re-institutionalisation is occurring, witnessed by the new forms of mutuality and collective action that are emerging.

'We are at the beginning of a period in which work and careers have the potential to be re-institutionalised.'

The reasons are not hard to find. Many workers have experienced the de-institutionalisation of work as being profoundly destabilising. They have sought solace, comfort and support in associations and networks populated by co-workers who share their knowledge and experience.

Other forms of collective action are on the rise. After a generation of decline in union membership and participation, the numbers of members have begun to rise once again – albeit from a small base.

We are at the beginning of a period in which work and careers have the potential to be re-institutionalised. This does not mean that we are witnessing a turning back of the clock – a wholesale reversion to standardised linear careers over which organisations and employers take prime responsibility and lead the way. Far from it. But the current trends do demand a response from organisations.

Organisational engagement

These recent shifts require a new kind of organisational engagement. Unless organisations engage, and inspire, the new breed of worker, they will fail to close the culture gap that is opening up between large organisations and the DIY economy.

There are hard economic reasons why they must do this.

At the moment, organisations have not harnessed the knowledge, creativity, innovation and experience of this new breed of workers, nor adapted mainstream organisational values to absorb and assimilate their values and experiences. Partly because of this, a DIY economy is already nascent.

At the most basic level, organisations must recruit and retain the most talented workers. This war for talent is already under way and it will become more competitive as time goes by. Far-sighted organisations have begun to offer career packages and benefits that encourage commitment and stability with which to attract and retain the best and most highly valued workers.

Only if mainstream work cultures show themselves to be receptive to diversity and to working with this new breed of worker will they be able to re-engage commitment among employees and prospective employees, rebuild trust and transform organisational cultures.

Perhaps most challenging of all, organisations will have to develop new kinds of relationships with their suppliers and partners in the elance economy – bringing them into the organisational extended family. Essential to every enterprise will be a vision of organisational development which treats these suppliers as partners and collaborators, and gives them a reason to buy into the organisation's vision, and to see that their own ambitions can be realised in partnership with the organisation. Organisations will have to spend time and energy engaging with their colleagues and associates in the e-lance economy and offering a convincing narrative about the new and emerging career patterns.

Conclusion

This is a radical kind of organisational engagement. Tomorrow's organisations will increasingly be 'employing organisations' dependent on a network of collaborators in the growing elance economy. But the power balance is likely to shift. They will have to sell themselves to a new breed of workers who will need to be won over.

And if they don't begin to take responsibility for their role in integrating and creating a new institutional framework within which individuals, in partnerships with organisations, can reconstruct career pathways, the consequences are likely to be negative – not just for the organisation, but for the national economy.

◘ Put simply, in an increasingly globalised knowledge economy, it is essential that organisations are recruiting and working with the most diverse knowledge pool at their disposal and are able to trust, motivate and engage these workers in the value-creation process.

◘ Already blue-chip companies are organising themselves around a strong central hub and are increasingly reliant on a network of suppliers, contractors and elancers. How they manage these workers is likely to become critical by 2050.

◘ At the moment, too few organisations are engaging in a dialogue about the future of careers, and as a consequence are giving the new generation very little reason to commit to or buy into large organisations.

◘ Such an approach is likely to lead to more and more individuals' opting out of mainstream organisations and going it alone – preferring the DIY economy over large organisations.

◘ The scene will then be set for an anti-career culture, and the growth of an elance economy which has a monopoly on creativity, innovation and diversity, and of which the knowledge capital – like its working style – is increasingly mobile.

◘ For organisations that depend on building and sustaining knowledge pools for future value creation, this scenario is one to be avoided at all costs.

Bruce Tulgan is an American business thinker who has clients all over the world. He is the founder of RainmakerThinking, Inc.® (www.rainmakerthinking.com) in New Haven, Connecticut, USA, a management-skills and career-skills training firm.

Bruce has written many books including *Winning the Talent Wars* (NB Books, UK, 2001), *Managing Generation X* (Capstone, UK, 1996), and *Work This Way* (Capstone, UK, 1998). In addition, Bruce is the author of a series of managers' pocket guides and training programmes published by HRD Press.

Before founding RainmakerThinking in 1993, Bruce practised law on Wall Street. He graduated with high honours from Amherst College and received his law degree from New York University. Bruce continues his lifelong study of Okinawan Uechi Ryu Karate Do and holds a fourth-degree black belt.

3 | Creating the customised career

Bruce Tulgan

In this highly interdependent, rapidly changing world, there are so many variables beyond our direct control – geopolitics, national politics, local politics, nature, market shifts around the globe, changes in particular industries ranging from new competitors to new inventions. Of course the list goes on. And all of this uncertainty has been with us for quite some time. Lately, however, uncertainty has become widely recognised as a default presumption. What does this all mean for employers, employees, and managers (the critical players who are stuck in the middle)?

For more than a decade, employers have been responding to these factors by seeking much greater organisational flexibility. Re-engineering is increasing speed and efficiency with improved systems and technology. Companies in every industry are redesigning the way work is done. Work systems, which in some cases have been in place for decades, are being dismantled and refashioned to improve flexibility, efficiency, and effectiveness. The challenge for employers over the next decade is to improve systems, practices and competencies in order to become even more flexible than they already are.

Using different generations as a lens through which to see the future

Although demographers differ over exact definitions, most experts agree that there are four distinct generations working side-by-side today. Let's look at each generation very briefly:

- *The 'Silent Generation', born before 1946, comprising roughly 10 per cent of today's workforce.* The workforce is ageing as the population ages and as employers lure those of traditional retirement age to work longer. Years of experience have taught Silents to rely on tried, true, and tested ways of doing things, and many would still agree, 'If it's not broken, don't fix it.' Silents still favour established systems, policies and procedures. They like the old rules. After years of working under command-and-control management, Silents are experiencing a radical change in the new workplace. Silents respond best to leaders and managers who respectfully assert their authority and demonstrate a clear track record of success.

- *The 'Baby Boomers', born between 1946 and 1964, comprising roughly 45 per cent of today's workforce.* Boomers, in their vast numbers, will make up the next wave of the ageing workforce. They paid their dues and climbed the ladder under the old rules and are currently to be found operating amidst constant downsizing, restructuring, and re-engineering. Boomers still pride themselves on their ability to survive 'sink or swim' management, but fewer today are willing to keep up the frenetic pace. Boomer women led the charge for workplace flexibility, and now many Boomers have caught on to the free-agent mindset. Boomers respond best to leaders and managers who listen attentively to their input and include them in decision-making, while challenging them to keep growing.

- *'Generation X', born between 1965 and 1977, comprising roughly 30 per cent of today's workforce.* When Generation X-ers hit the workforce in the late 1980s, they were typecast as disloyal job-hoppers who didn't want to pay their dues and wanted everything their own way. But X-ers formed the vanguard of the free-agent workforce. Now X-ers are growing up and moving into positions of supervisory responsibility and leadership, but they are not settling down. X-ers remain cautious and they know that their security rests in staying on the cutting edge. Always in a hurry, X-ers will often sidestep rules as they push for results. They're willing to take risks to keep learning and innovating. X-ers respond best to leaders and managers who spend time coaching, clarifying the day-to-day bargain at work, and giving credit for results achieved.

- *'Generation Y', born between 1978 and 1986, comprising roughly 15 per cent of today's workforce.* This is the first wave of the 'Echo-boom' or the 'Millennial' generation. Coming of age during the most expansive economy in the last 30 years, Gen Y-ers are the children of Baby Boomers and the optimistic, upbeat younger siblings of Gen X-ers. The first cohort of truly 'global citizens', they are socially conscious and volunteer-minded. Gen Y-ers have been told by parents, teachers, counsellors, and churches that they can do anything – and they believe it. They are poised to be the most demanding generation in history. Gen Y-ers respond best to leaders and managers who respect them as individuals and keep them engaged with speed, customisation and interactivity.

One of the most important things we've learned is that the clash between generations playing out in the workplace today is not merely a matter of young versus old. This clash pits the old-fashioned expectations, values and practices of stability against the new reality of constant change and the consequent need for agility.

The transformation of organisational structure

Throughout most of the industrial era and until recently, the dominant staffing model for most employers was based on long-term employment relationships with long-term employees. People were expected to start in entry-level positions appropriate to their skills and credentials and then, over time, move their way up the ladder. The key features of this model were stability and predictability. Staffing strategy was all about planning for openings in an otherwise static organisation chart. With slight adjustments, the positions on the chart remained the same – like the positions in a sports team. Only, the people who filled those positions would change periodically – like the players in a sports team.

Successful organisations in the future will all share the ability to adapt rapidly to new circumstances – whether they are unexpectedly upcoming market opportunities or suddenly vanishing market opportunities. Depending on the circumstances, staffing may have to expand rapidly, or contract rapidly or both at the same time. Certain skills may be required all of a sudden and others, just as suddenly, may be no longer necessary. In the new economy, staffing needs will be in constant flux. Employers will gear their staffing strategies around coping with this reality.

In order to meet unpredictable staffing needs on an as-needed basis, employers will let go of rigid organisation structures and employment models. The attitude will be 'Whatever it takes to get the work done, do it, no matter how much it stretches your current business practices', and this will explode the organisation chart. Several leading researchers at the Stanford Business School have confirmed that when companies get locked into a particular way of organising their workforce, they limit the options of managers trying to respond to shifting demands in the marketplace.[1] Successful organisations in the future will not limit their options and will create more ways to employ people. They will use a mix of contractors, employees, part-timers and some-timers. Those organisations that don't want the 'trouble' of flexible work arrangements will find it hard to hold on to talented people. As one executive I recently interviewed said:

I've heard a number of stories where a really great staff member is leaving and willing to work part-time in a consulting role but the management in their group refuse. They usually say that 'It would be bad for morale to let a former employee make more money by contracting back.' They just don't get it.

> '*Successful organisations in the future will not limit their options and will create more ways to employ people.*'

The approach of successful organisations will be one where a team of technical specialists work together to solve the problem. The organisation will take the lead in guiding the group's design solution and will help employees get work that meets their goals.

Reinventing long-term employment as fluid and flexible

We can reinvent long-term employment, and thus save it, by having a wide repertoire of ways to employ people. Actually, we shall need an infinite number. This outcome is inevitable in a free market for talent. Think about it. In a free market, you get what you can negotiate. That's it. Every negotiation turns out differently, depending upon the value proposition at stake, the skill of the people negotiating, and the degree to which each party can compromise.

If every condition of employment – not just pay, but schedule, duration of employment, location, assignments, and so on – is on the table, the negotiating position as a manager is stronger, not weaker. Instead of negotiating with their hands tied, managers will make the best deal that makes sense in every situation. Ultimately, the more terms of employment are on, the more ways there are to employ people, the more ways there will be to get the work done and to retain people.

The flip side is this. In a free-market environment, the best people at every level will be able to negotiate the best deals. And that's the way it

should be. In fact, the very best people at every level can already just about name their own terms, as long as they can get all the work done. And as long as they can get all the work done, why shouldn't they name their terms? That's a pretty good deal, for everyone involved.

Building the dream job through customisation

Based on our research, these are the five non-financial factors of an employment relationship that people care the most about:

◘ when they work (schedule)

◘ where they work (location)

◘ what they do (tasks and responsibilities)

◘ who they work with

◘ what they are (or are not) learning on the job.

When people are free to customise these factors, they design dream jobs. The dream job factors are the most valuable currency an employer can possibly offer.

To have long-term employment relationships with the very best people, organisations will learn to employ people in many, many different ways. They will employ people wherever, whenever, and however they are willing and able to add the value. When a valuable person goes to the trouble to customise his work situation, negotiating special arrangements with the organisation, his manager and his co-workers, his stake in the position grows tremendously. His investment in the organisation, his commitment, his willingness to deliver results grows. Why? 'This is my dream job,' he will say. That's a job worth keeping.

Organisations will regularly assess and reassess the people who work for them. They will ask how transparent their value is to themselves – how transparent their value is to the organisation. They will implement processes that discern exactly what every person is worth in order to be able to negotiate effectively. Leaders and managers who are willing and able to negotiate on these factors can help people wrap the work that needs to get done around the kind of life they want to have. In this way, employers can often turn the reasons why employees are unhappy and unproductive into reasons why they will stay for the foreseeable future and work harder than ever before.

As the demand for work–life balance accelerates, the pressure on employers will continue to grow. The one-size-fits-all career path is now the single greatest obstacle to reliable staffing because the best people simply won't work for you if they can't get their personal needs met. Organisations in the future will break free from this mould.

The alternative career path trend

Beyond flexible work arrangements such as flexitime and telecommuting, more and more organisations are developing alternative career paths that allow talented people to step outside the organisation chart and still remain within the organisation. This option has come to be known as 'career downshifting'.

The big problem with 'career downshifting' is that although it does give talented people new options, these options require a person to opt out of the fast track – the path to the greatest status and rewards. This is easiest to see in professional services firms with partnership structures because they make the choice most explicit. One young lawyer I spoke with recently told me:

They are losing so many people, they are creating an option to work three days a week, but if you do that, you are pretty much saying, 'I don't want to be a partner.'

In a growing number of professional services firms, there is no need to wonder at this. They have created what they explicitly refer to as 'non-partner' tracks. Typically, those on the 'non-partner' tracks are required to develop a deep technical expertise in some area and are then asked to manage a specific area of responsibility – usually an assignment that affords the employee greater control over his schedule and location.[2]

The non-partner track initiatives, like other work–life balance initiatives, represent real progress in the move toward career customisation. But they are often precisely the exceptions designed to perpetuate the rule. The underlying message is this:

If you are a real superstar, one of us, the kind of person likely to reach the pinnacle of success here (the top of the ladder), you are going to pay your dues like the rest of us did. Yes, there are flexible options – for the people who can't cut it the old-fashioned way.

Employers with this view are still betting that, faced with the choice, most of the best people will choose the fast track and many others will stay and choose the slower track because it's the best choice available to them. But it won't be for long.

A senior partner at Cap Gemini Ernst & Young recently told me that his firm now operates on the assumption that all of its employees are volunteers to the enterprise. For that reason, the firm now maintains an entire database of best practices and success stories regarding alternative career paths that may be available to 'volunteers' within the firm.

Far more ambitious, however, is Cap Gemini Ernst & Young's impressive role-based reconfiguration of its entire organisation structure[3] – an effort that I was thrilled to contribute to by working with its human resources team. In place of its traditional 'up or out' structure – five ascending levels on the consulting hierarchy leading to partner – Cap Gemini Ernst & Young has now put in place a far more flexible structure involving 15 different roles that consultants must apply for specifically on each new consulting engagement. The roles are defined not by level but rather by *exactly what the person is expected to do* during a particular assignment.

In other words, the roles are defined by the work, not the job. This structure allows for much more fluid career paths because individuals may apply for any role on any project, moving from one role to another as projects end and new ones begin. By reviewing the detailed role profiles, individuals can see what competencies they have to have to be accepted for a particular role and perform successfully in it. A person can thus focus his or her professional learning at any given point on the role he or she aspires to play – in other words, train for the mission. Cap Gemini Ernst & Young now provides role-based learning maps to enable individuals to train for each mission more effectively. The system promotes clear expectations every step of the way, and helps managers more accurately evaluate performance against specific work objectives.

Even outside the new role-based structure, Cap Gemini Ernst & Young provides unique opportunities for very talented people who wish to step off the traditional path but stay on the fast track. One opportunity available to highly skilled consultants is to work in what the firm calls its Advance Development Centers (ADCs) located throughout the world and dedicated to providing clients with high-level technology solutions – web-based, client-server-based, and so on – to complex business challenges. For the most part, ADC consultants do not travel to client sites but work instead on high-level assignments within the centers. Another high-level career alternative at the firm is what Cap Gemini Ernst & Young calls Global Operate (GO). In an innovative combination of traditional outsourcing and consulting, the firm's GO employees take long-term responsibility for one or more of a client's business processes, such as managing a complex integrated database or an e-commerce platform. Consultants working in GO environments typically look more like, and in some cases become, employees of the client organisation and are located on-site on a relatively permanent basis, eliminating the constant travel element of the traditional consulting role.

By abandoning its obsolete organisation chart, Cap Gemini Ernst & Young has opened a world of possibilities for its 'volunteers' (employees) and given itself a huge strategic advantage in recruiting and retaining the best consulting talent. Every track at the firm is now a fast track, and as a result, high-level talent can negotiate custom work arrangements without being forced to downshift. Of course, the competition will follow suit in short order.

Total customisation

Recently, I met with three of Deloitte Consulting's top leaders. They had asked me to come in and help them prepare for a long-range strategic planning meeting the senior partners were about to have. How could they stem the tide of good people flowing out of the firm?

I told them bluntly that they should abandon the up-or-out career path, and I continued:

Let your best people work wherever they want, whenever they want, however they want. Just negotiate on an ongoing basis a market-based deal that makes sense. Buy their results on a short-term basis, on whatever terms you and they can negotiate. Don't be locked into one rigid way of employing people.

When they assured me they already had alternative career paths, I urged them to think about their best people.

It is your best people who want the fast track to authority and compensation, but they are also the people with the most negotiating power. If you are offering people the old-fast-track or the slow-track, that is no option for ambitious success-minded people. They want to do the fast track their own way. And if you don't let them do it here, they will do it somewhere else.

'Every track at the firm is now a fast track.'

At this point one of them said, musingly:

If we are going to create this kind of flexibility – work wherever, whenever, however you want – we should do that for the senior partners, not for the junior consultants.

This, I believe, was the genesis of Deloitte's 'Senior Leaders Program' which has received a lot of attention in the business media. It is a bid to retain some of the firm's best and brightest by allowing them to customise their careers so they can work wherever, whenever and however they are able to add value in the firm – but only the best and brightest over the age of 50. It is reserved, like so many other privileges and rewards, for those in the firm who have paid their dues and climbed the ladder in tribute to the rites of the established hierarchy.

Here's the thinking. The typical retirement age for consultants is around 50 (because the work is so gruelling). That's when pensions vest and that's when people have usually had just about enough. With the ageing of the firm's population (the number of partners reaching age 50 is doubling over the next five years) and the general drain of talent afflicting the firm, Deloitte decided to retain some of their best talent the only way possible. 'Restructure your job any way you want,' they are saying to their top partners. 'Create your dream job.' And it's working. After all, who would quit a dream job? Now instead of losing many of their best and most seasoned partners, the firm will keep them indefinitely. They will be called upon when and where they are needed and they will do the work at hand if they feel like it, negotiating appropriate fees for their services on an ongoing basis. What a great way to stem the tide of talent flowing out of your firm.

Be a change leader

How can we create a workplace where the customised dream job is the norm?

- ◪ Learn from the different perspectives and needs of the different generations in the workplace today. They are all experiencing the profound changes differently. And their experiences are a reflection of the fundamental tension in the workplace of the future between the old and the new.

- ◪ Start planning long-term relationships with valued contributors of all ages around each individual's unique life plan (not the other way around).

- ◪ Help people to play to their strengths and interests, and to develop along those lines, and to continue adding more and more value. Encourage them to 'just grow' in their dream jobs – working for you.

- ◪ Forget 'That's not the way we do things around here' and start doing things that way. You may have to be the one to break new ground. So what? Take it one day at a time. As you are negotiating short-term pay for performance deals for the results you need, you should be negotiating the conditions of employment as well.

- ◪ Customise a deal for every person – value for value – around the roles they actually play (their tasks, responsibilities and projects) rather than around positions on an organisational chart.

At the very least, whenever you can possibly do it, grant people the slight adjustments they request. Even small efforts at customisation go a long way. The best people will climb over each other to work for you. Spurn the old-fashioned rites of passage. You are not a feudal lord. You are a free-market manager. Play that role aggressively and you are going to start winning the talent wars

References

1 James N. Baron, Diane M. Burton and Michael T. Hannon (forthcoming), *The Road Taken: Origins and evolution of employment systems in emerging companies*, Industrial and Corporate Change. Michael T. Hannan, Diane M. Burton and James M. Baron (forthcoming), *Inertia and Change in the Early Years: Employment relations in young high-technology firms*, Industrial and Corporate Change.

2 'Managing retention at Deloitte Consulting', *Journal of Management Consulting*, Volume 10, No. 3, May 1999; p55. 'Brain drain', *Business Week*, Jennifer Reingold with Diane Brady, 20 September 1999.

3 Rhonda Fleming, Assistant Director in the Centre for People Process Innovation at Cap Gemini Ernst & Young, provided much of the details of their role-based system and other career alternatives.
'Will retirement centers turn into hiring halls?', *Wall Street Journal*, 29 February 2000, pA1.

Ralph Tribe is Vice-President, Human Resources, for Getty Images Inc. [NASDAQ: GETY], a global company with 2001 revenues in excess of $450 million, rated as one of the top 50 e-commerce businesses in the world.

Ralph started his career in sales with Reed International Publishing and then moved into human resource management with Railtrack, where he was part of a project team that successfully took this organisation from being an interesting idea to a fully-operational *FTSE* 100 business in almost the blink of an eye.

After a period in consultancy with Qtab Ltd, where he specialised in delivering business-critical HR strategies in hyper-growth and turn-around environments, Ralph joined DA Consulting Group as European Head of HR. DA took on the mighty 'Big Five' to become European market leader within their niche, primarily by developing one of the most compelling employer brands in a market where recruiting and retaining the best was the only way to get to the top and stay there.

Ralph joined Getty Images in 1999, where he is now engaged in the race to revolutionise the 'visual content' market space for creative, publishing and editorial customers around the world. Once again, this is a market in which skills are scarce, and in which recruiting and retaining the best people is *the* differentiating factor.

4 | The self-managed career – the key to the future can be found in the past

Ralph Tribe

Just imagine...

- Imagine if sometime this century some individual or some organisation invented some product or concept that could potentially transform the life of every single person on the planet. It would likely be simple for ease of use and adoption, capable of mass distribution, be priced at low cost for easy accessibility, and of course, would arrive as a flat-pack or for self-assembly (like so many things these days!).

- Imagine then, if, once the product was invented and launched, it transpired that the critical tools to enable the final step to using this amazing life-enhancing item – the self-assembly instructions and toolkit, say – were not being marketed with the same vigour, nor being made easily available to customers.

- And imagine that this then led to a bizarre situation in which customers didn't necessarily realise that the product *was* in fact a self-assembly kit, and that it required to be

constructed in a particular way to deliver the promise.

This is not a dream … In fact, although it may seem just a little too far-fetched, the bad news is that this scenario has already happened. The good news is that it's not too late to relaunch this wonder product. The frightening possibility is that if we don't, the consequences may be serious – very serious.

The self-managed career

The wonder-product is the self-managed career. This fundamentally important concept fully took root in the early part of the 1990s when, at the end of the last recession, it became alarmingly clear that the concept of the organisation as the principal sponsor of its employees' careers was not sustainable in an environment of increasing change and uncertainty.

The self-managed career did come with clear instructions and self-assembly toolkit (once). With the organisation at that time playing, at least in theory, an enabling role in career management in preference to a driving role, people required clear guidance on how to transform their lives using this new concept. Such guidance and the toolkit came in the simple form of a 'self-marketing framework'. Engagingly straightforward, it worked on the basis that in a 'free' market for jobs and careers, individuals should view themselves as a unique 'product' and market themselves accordingly.

'UK plc would benefit from significantly enhanced productivity and competitiveness, and society at large would benefit from a generally happier, more empowered population.'

The product had 'features' in the form of skills and knowledge, and more importantly, 'benefits', which resulted from the successful application of these skills and knowledge in practice. These could be marketed and sold to employers, and used to differentiate oneself from the next person in a vast pool of labour. Careers could be driven by developing new skill and knowledge features, applying these to achieve greater and greater outcomes, and marketing these potential benefits to employers when necessary to reach the next stage of one's aspirational pathway.

There was a huge potential up-side to be gained from this new approach, both for individuals and for organisations. The promise of ever-increasing personal marketability based on an expanding

personal portfolio of delivered benefits would lead to an increased motivation towards outcome over input.

In this environment, individuals would find a clearer focus for their skills and knowledge – an increased potential for their features in terms of marketability, job choices, career, wealth and, ultimately, personal fulfilment. As a result, they would be more achievement-oriented, and in turn they would become more fulfilled as a result of their achievements.

Organisations would clearly benefit from mass increases in the levels of personal effectiveness in the workplace delivered by this approach to career. UK plc would benefit from significantly enhanced productivity and competitiveness in both the private and public sectors, and society at large would benefit from a generally happier, motivated and more empowered population.

I said, this is *not* a dream …

Interestingly, this idea is more than 10 years old – yet when one reads it now it *still* feels like a futuristic scenario. One has to wonder, why does it still feel so far away when so much is already in place to enable this paradigm shift? There is no doubt that the switch in responsibility has taken place, creating a more open careers market. Furthermore, there are clearly individuals out there – albeit a very small minority – who have fully embraced the concept of self-marketing and the pursuit of outcome over input to great effect.

An obsession with 'features'

In truth, we're all playing our part in holding it back – all of us, comprising:

◧ individuals

◧ employers

◧ 'career brokers'

◧ the government, the state.

In general, we all got part-way through the instructions but consistently failed to read through to the second half.

Collectively we have fallen into the age-old product-development trap – a focus on features rather than on benefits. In terms of the self-managed career, we have become obsessed with the skills and knowledge part while we generally ignore the critically important application of these features to deliver benefit to others (employers, customers, etc). In the careers market, we typically focus on what the person looks like in terms of their features rather than how they have used them to deliver something beneficial.

If you don't believe this, consider the current behaviours of the major players in today's careers market.

Individuals

Take a look at almost any CV. Ninety-nine per cent of CVs still show just qualifications, skills, job duties, positions held and previous employers. Rarely is there a mention of how the individual's employment has benefited the organisation he or she has worked for.

Thinking beyond features can be painful. Often it brings with it the distressing realisation that although one has developed all sorts of skills and knowledge, one has not in fact added much value to date. If a person gets even this far, it's a breakthrough, but then the early discomfort of change becomes an issue. Focusing one's efforts on delivering benefits rather than on developing features is ultimately more rewarding but initially more challenging. It requires an individual to experiment, to take more risks and to work further outside his or her comfort zone – and as we all know, change comes with a certain degree of pain for most people.

For the few who successfully make *this* shift, the final hurdle is how to apply these marketing concepts in the skilful management of their careers. It's well understood that most products – even those with great features and a superb track-record of delivering benefits – still have to contend with a natural product life-cycle. There comes a point where people have to innovate in order to keep moving forward, or they stagnate. In the careers market this equates to an individual's getting to the high point of the initial career pathway but wanting to do something fundamentally different thereafter in order to continue feeling fulfilled – perhaps, for example, by moving from a corporate career to starting up a business for oneself.

Sadly, most people who try to make a fundamental career change fail and return to their initial career pathway. This is often because they forget to be innovative in their personal product plan and/or the way that they market themselves. For example, a senior manager who leaves his or her large organisation to go it alone as, say, a management consultant, is by no means guaranteed success in the new situation – particularly if he or she positions his or her benefits in the very same way that previously delivered a flourishing career in the corporate environment. With products, differentiation is key to success, and the self-managed career is no different.

> **'Most people who try to make a fundamental career change fail and return to their initial career pathway. This is often because they forget to be innovative.'**

Employers

Employers also play a key role in either holding this concept back, or letting it fly. At the moment, probably unwittingly, they're holding it back. Take a look at any job advertisement. Recruiters talk a good talk, but as often as not fail to show what benefits they expect from the advertised role, and rarely challenge candidates to apply with details of

how they can specifically add value. Employers compound the issue by selling themselves to candidates as poorly as candidates sell themselves to employers, as if the features of their organisation alone are enough to constitute a compelling offer.

Most employers also shy away from the full-on promotion of 'marketability' within their workforce. They worry that the more marketable their employees are, the more expensive they will become or the easier they will find it to leave. For the most part, employers are still missing the point that from a value perspective their most effective people are their least expensive, whatever you have to pay them, and that the more an organisation encourages and enables its people to deliver maximum benefit, the more likely they are to stay – why should they leave?

Career-brokers

These are the companies that offer products and services within the careers market, and of course profit from it. Head-hunters, recruitment consultants, recruitment- and career-portals – all of these groups occupy a space where they could be commercially threatened or excited by the idea of greater individual empowerment in the market. In one scenario these middlemen get cut out of the equation when individuals take a view that they could do a better job of driving their own career by bringing their marketing 'in-house'. In another, the career-brokers benefit because the whole market gets lifted beyond the current sea of blandness as personal differentiation becomes a genuine focus.

The current situation, however, is one in which the career-brokers are, for the most part, doing little to challenge the status quo. The traditional features-oriented approach is still very much in evidence.

◨ Head-hunters typically do little to influence their clients to think beyond a turgid features-laden brief, so the same old people tend to float around in each industry. Potential achievers from outside still face artificial and irrelevant barriers to entering new job markets.

◨ The recruitment agencies still work off CV databases built on the tired principle of matching individuals' features to job features. These databases simply cannot search out achievements, yet they are the starting-point for most matching reports.

◨ Similarly, recruitment-portals – which increasingly claim to offer an exciting alternative – actually offer nothing new. They continue to rely upon search engines that cannot qualify a potential candidate on the basis of potential value-added because, despite huge technological advances, computers still cannot think conceptually (yet).

The government, the state

The state's greatest contribution to the careers market could be to provide education programmes that first and foremost focus on giving individuals the investigative and analytical skills to match inputs with outcomes. Benefit must be the principal objective, rather than feature development. Imagine the impact if the general population was attuned to the concept of personal effectiveness from the age of 3 onwards!

Disappointingly, everything from the national curriculum to vocational qualifications appears to be built on the principle of input first, outcome second. What is perhaps most unnerving is the sense that so long as we develop the skills and knowledge features, the benefits will *automatically* follow – despite the well-known fact that competence doesn't necessarily equal effectiveness.

Take a look at any NVQ. The assessment criteria inevitably focus on what an individual can do rather than whether the intended benefits of being able to do it are actually delivered. This is akin to testing whether a trainee chef can bake a particular cake but not what it actually tastes like! Is it any wonder that Britain continues to lag behind its neighbours in terms of public service provision and commercial competitiveness?

Evolution, anarchy or extinction – we have a choice?

So where do we go from here? Who goes first?

> *'Employers now have everything to gain by embracing and promoting the full package, and are at increasing risk of losing everything if they don't.'*

Well, at this point it's probably employers who can make the greatest contribution towards relaunching the concept of the self-managed career and genuinely unleashing its full potential this time. As we know, the employers have taken the first step of relinquishing control of the careers market. If we could now stop deluding ourselves that the work is complete just because the *basic* concept is embedded, we could get busy reintroducing the self-marketing instruction manual and tool-set. We've reached an inflection point. Employers now have everything to gain by embracing and promoting the *full* package, and are at increasing risk of losing everything if they don't!

If you think this is an overstatement, or unnecessarily alarmist, we haven't talked about Generation X yet, nor Generation Y. There are signs that these populations are growing more and more disillusioned and alienated by work. They're savvy enough to realise that they have been left to get on with it, but they can't quite figure out why their progress isn't accelerating as expected. At this point their lives and careers are little more enriched than their parents'.

If the situation continues as it has been for the past 10 years, there will be an increasing divide between the small minority of successful 'careerists' who have the skills and knowledge *and* who are able to market the benefits they bring to organisations, and the masses of 'jobbers' who can't.

The marketing-savvy careerists will funnel all their activity into the ongoing release of value, and thereby move easily from opportunity to opportunity, maximising their learning and marketability, and hand-picking who they want to work for, *when* they want to work. Indeed, Generation X careerists may increasingly chose to move in and out of work in a dynamic fusion of work- and leisure-based projects. Most obviously, *they* will be in control. If fulfilment is a product of empowerment, they will be fulfilled.

Conversely, if disillusionment is the product of a lack of control and an increasing awareness of the shortfall between what is possible and one's own personal progress, then this is the jobbers' sad future. In the traditional economy the jobber was just about adequate, and the divide between the Haves and the Have-nots was not so great as to cause widespread alienation. However, in the connected economy of the future, where good information, applied knowledge and the ongoing development of intellectual capital are the principal requirements to survive, an organisation's success will depend on how many careerists they can attract, how many they can develop, and how many they can retain. Organisations that are most successful in their efforts to transform their jobbers into careerists will thrive. Those that fail to do so will find an ever-enlarging distance between their organisational goals and their people's ability or motivation to deliver them. These organisations will die.

If that sounds a little worrying, then consider Generation Y. Unlike Generation X, this group now entering the workplace do not necessarily regard capitalism as inherently desirable, nor do they necessarily believe that there is no better alternative.

For Generation X, maturity typically comes with the realisation that their youthful idealism was fine, but work can also provide fulfilment in its own right. At worst, work is a benign obligation that has to be fulfilled in a capitalist system in order that one can pay the bills while achieving fulfilment elsewhere. Generation Y, however, because they have an even higher expectation of what work should deliver and are also more inclined towards an alternative, may have a more radical response if work fails to deliver to their expectations. Imagine if, working in the interests of a perceived 'greater good', the careerists were to redirect their considerable talents towards corporate sabotage, while their jobbing comrades pursued an alternative path to fulfilment through political revolution!

Finally, let's spare a last thought for Generation Z. Right now they're still at school. But consider this wild possibility for a moment. If this group enters the workplace at the same time as technological progress delivers virtual reality to the masses, and it's a bad experience, then we may have a much more serious problem. Think about it. When gratification no longer has to be worked for but can be delivered instantly at the push of a button, work will simply *have* to offer so much more in order to provide a better alternative to the 'quick fix' of an artificial existence.

Extinction-level events presumably come in many shapes and sizes, but the most dangerous possibilities often start where you least expect them!

Salvation!

Salvation? Simple.

Give back the instructions and market the benefits of using them. The rest will follow.

Do it soon.

John Mockler is Head of Human Resources for Tate. He joined the galleries after leading the HR function at two of the country's largest teaching hospitals. Before this he worked for over 20 years in local government, dealing with general management, career development, recruitment and industrial relations. He has extensive experience and knowledge of successful change management within the public sector. John is also currently the Chair of the CIPD's Career Management and Counselling Forum, and in this capacity is a speaker at events across the country.

5 | Careers don't stop at 50 – where are the people for the future?

John Mockler

Whatever happened to career development?

There have been times over the past five years in particular when the notion of career development appears to have dropped off the employers' agenda and been replaced by self-directed career management – leaving it to high-flyers to forge their own path on a do-it-yourself basis. In practice, for many employers this usually means paying what it takes to get your competitors' best-qualified staff working for you. It makes sense. After all, those with ambition who want to develop their careers will certainly be looking for new opportunities elsewhere. Savings in training and development costs can offset the salaries they demand. Whenever there is economic slowdown, the first casualty is often the training and development budget, and so long as a steady supply of talent exists to feed demand, such a strategy will work for those organisations able to afford it. But career development is an investment for the future that we neglect at our peril.

With hindsight it was possible to see a crisis in career development coming. For some years articles about the demographic 'time-bomb' were a staple of the HR press. These tended to focus on the recruitment aspects of the issue and the need to develop stronger work-based learning provision to meet future needs. This was all good sense, but the reality was that the main beneficiaries of this training were graduates. We did not as a nation effectively address career development from a strategic perspective, embracing all the workforce and trying to develop their skills and experience to meet future needs, rather than relying on individual employers and their staff.

Defining what our future needs might be is not easy within the current employment market. Who could have predicted the existence of such jobs as 'website editor', or say now whether they will still be here in ten years' time? Who could have foreseen that the development of the Internet would be so fast that it now makes overwhelming economic sense for customer service support for a

38 | **The Future of Careers**

Careers don't stop at 50 – where are the people for the future?

client in Yorkshire to be provided in real time from an industrial estate in New Delhi? The reality for many workers is that they are embarking on a series of different careers – often sequential but sometimes parallel – over the course of their working lives. The sheer pace and degree of change means that we must now take a long hard look at what we mean by 'career development', how such varied experience can be mined for the benefit of the individual and his or her employer, and who the key players are.

Clearly, competition and securing optimum performance are paramount for success – although not at the expense of our seed-corn. But that is what has happened. The consequences of our failure to predict and anticipate the obvious effects of throttling back investment in training and career development in the past are now coming home to roost. The effect can be seen most clearly in the public sector where the ability to buy one's way out of the problem is severely limited. The present shortage of suitably qualified staff in sufficient numbers to meet society's demands must inevitably diminish everyone's competitive edge.

The public sector crisis

The public sector is highly rated for training and development[1] and has often acted in the past as a feeder to satisfy private sector recruitment problems. It is very different now. It would be unwise to claim that the current shortages of key public staff – teachers, doctors, social workers, train drivers, and so on – is a result of failure to support effective career development. It is far more likely that negative reporting, poor public image, low morale, seemingly endless change, and (in the south-east) housing costs, combined with steadily rising client expectations that cannot be satisfied within available resources, have all played their part. Nevertheless, this is the result:

◘ teachers – 31,000 will be needed over the next three years.[2] This is despite the fact that there are now 12,000 more teachers in our schools than there were in 1998.[3]

◘ nurses – There is a potential shortfall of 57,000 by 2005.[4]

◘ police – More than 4,000 are needed now.[5]

◘ doctors – There are 2,464 GP vacancies now, and a requirement of 10,000 extra family doctors if the government is to achieve its plan.[6]

We have to ask where we shall get the people to fill all our other jobs if the younger workers are recruited to fill long-term career jobs such as teaching and medicine. Unless we can answer that question and get the new recruits, the present crisis can only continue and, taking the age-profile of local government staff as an example, probably get worse (see Table 1).

The Future of Careers | **39**

Careers don't stop at 50 – where are the people for the future?

Part of the answer has to be that we must change our perceptions of the mature worker. In *Ageism: Too costly to ignore* (Employers' Forum on Age, 2001), Sean Rickard concludes:

If we do not succeed as a society in reducing the numbers of people over 50 who are not actively engaged in the economy, we are likely to suffer a cumulative annual loss of GDP and an associated fall in living standards…

Capitalising on past investment

Traditional models of career development saw someone entering an organisation and – with their employers' support and guidance – eventually acquiring the skills and experience necessary to undertake higher-level work. Progression was usually measured through financial success and promotion – onwards and upwards. The employer

Table 1 | Age-profile of local government staff in 1999.

Age	Percentage representation in	
	local government	the whole economy
Under 25	7	16
25–34	19	26
35–49	45	36
50–54	14	11
55+	15	11
	100	100

Source: Labour Force Survey, Summer 1999.

was often large enough to offer internal secondments and sponsor study for formal qualifications. The payoff in terms of reduced staff turnover and an increasingly skilled and experienced workforce made such investment worthwhile.

It is doubtful that this ideal symbiotic relationship ever existed for long outside the imagination of personnel departments. However, there can be little doubt that the dramatic shake-up of industry from the 1970s onwards meant that such an organic approach to career development was inappropriate and too long-term to be relevant outside large highly-structured public and private sector organisations, such as the Civil Service. In response to this the concept of self-directed career management became more important. But the older worker, often a repository of key organisational knowledge, did not generally move on and in many cases was made redundant as retrenchment occurred. We lost the investment.

In a youth-centred culture we have to ensure that careers no longer stop or start to slow down at 50. We must keep the older workers working and develop them further. Although it is surprising that the economic case for using older staff has yet to gain wider recognition, some far-sighted employers have recognised it and have already staked out their claims in this part of the recruitment market. A visit to the Employers Forum on Age website (www.efa-agediversity.org.uk) will provide relevant case studies.

40 | **The Future of Careers**

Careers don't stop at 50 – where are the people for the future?

Recent initiatives

Changes in the recruitment and retirement policies of stores and supermarkets such as B&Q and Sainsbury's are not designed simply to reflect their customer-base. They are also a pragmatic response to their need to tap into overlooked pools of talent in advance of their competitors. Using mature staff in high-profile consumer advertising makes sound marketing sense, but there is more for them to do than stacking shelves as they do in the TV advert. Nationwide's experience is especially interesting. They recruited IT trainees in their 40s, taking the organisation from a position in which 71 per cent of IT staff were in the 26 to 45 age-bracket to a situation in which 12 per cent are now under 26 and 22 per cent are over 45. The extent to which these people will be able to develop a career with their employers remains to be seen, but the shortage of IT staff generally gives them opportunities to move on if they wish.

The lasting shortage of young recruits is now forcing us all to look again at older workers and build strategies to attract and retain them. Key to these strategies will be an approach to career development that does not focus solely on the 'upwards and onwards' principles of the past. It must allow the individual to be flexible in deploying his or her talents to best effect in responding to the employer's needs. The older worker comes with a well-tested range of skills and experience which offers a reduced learning curve and an ability to hit the ground running. It also affords opportunities for the transfer of skills to younger workers, thus improving their career development.

Developing older workers for the future

So how can older workers be developed? I suggest that we start by looking at outplacement counselling practice. The key start in effective outplacement is a thorough analysis of the skills and experiences of the client. This takes us into a process involving three steps:

Step 1

First we need to identify:

◘ their total employment history

◘ their skills, both formal and practical, acquired inside and outside work

◘ their expectations for the future – these are likely to be very different from the 25- to 35-year-old workers'

◘ their perceptions of opportunities within the workplace. This may require a review of retirement policies to shift to flexible individual retirement planning. We're going to have to do it by 2006 anyway, so why not do it now? Recent press reports about future pension prospects means that some of our older staff will want to work on past 65.

The Future of Careers | 41

Careers don't stop at 50 – where are the people for the future?

People value the skills, experience, and status they have acquired over many years, and knowing that their employer also values and can use them is an important motivational factor. This leads to:

Step 2

Identify and agree:

- where these skills and experience can be deployed most effectively – this implies a willingness to redesign or mould jobs to suit the individual

- how we can transfer these skills and experience to younger workers in the course of their own career development

- processes by which to facilitate this – perhaps mentoring, coaching, shadowing, or similar initiatives.

Again this provides powerful motivation for the older worker – passing on skills and practical knowledge to the succeeding 'generation'.

Step 3

Identify and agree:

- additional individual training and development needs – these can range from basic IT through to adult apprenticeships or NVQs

> *'People value the skills, experience, and status they have acquired over many years, and knowing that their employer also values and can use them is an important motivational factor'*

- how their working time will be structured. Does the job have to be full-time? Can we support flexible working?

Charles Handy's *The Third Age* saw the older worker as becoming involved in community activities, providing key support for voluntary groups and charities, and filling gaps that were not covered by the state. Can we support this and perhaps incorporate it into our social responsibility activities?

The stakeholders

The potential labour shortage means that we are now in a position where career development is too important to be left solely to employers and individuals. There are three major stakeholders: the government, the employer, and the employee.

- *The government* must take a more active role in supporting employer initiatives. Reintroducing the Individual Learning Accounts in England would be a good start. Even better would be financial support for employers wishing to start up mature apprenticeships. Better still would be a change in Inland Revenue rules that prevent workers from taking part of their company pension yet

42 | **The Future of Careers**

Careers don't stop at 50 – where are the people for the future?

continuing to work part-time for the same employer. The *Guardian* (17 November 2001) estimated that this single change alone would enable 3 million more people to work. It would also retain the benefit of the investment we have already made in these people.

■ *The employer* must be persuaded away from the outmoded thinking in our perception of what makes an effective worker. We must be more willing to adapt our current practices to meet the needs of staff. Flexible working is not simply about helping people with carer responsibilities. It is a key tool in ensuring that we retain them and keep them working for us, not for our competitors. Above all, we must be willing to see the potential in our longer-serving staff and ensure that their skills and experience are passed on to colleagues.

■ *The employee*, especially the older worker who wants and expects to see his or her work experience valued, must also accept that the concept that 'knowledge is power' is outmoded. Employees' true value to their employer derives from their willingness to share their skills and knowledge with colleagues.

Our older workers represent a major underutilised national asset. Circumstance may be forcing us to consider a wider age-balance in our workforces, but we must also develop this asset. Successful development, in my view, lies in reaffirming truths that in recent years have tended to become obscured:

The older worker is:

■ not over the hill – there is no biological evidence to suggest that an older worker is mentally slower, and in fact some research shows that he or she may have greater learning capacity

■ a valuable repository of skills and knowledge to be tapped for the benefit of our younger workers

■ not incapable of dealing with change – on the contrary, an older worker's greater experience of work and of life in general may well equip him or her to deal with it more effectively

■ eminently worth developing throughout the remainder of his or her working life.

References

1 SOCPO report, 2001.

2 House of Commons Library.

3 DfEE response to BBC News comment, August 2001.

4 Royal College of Nursing, 2001.

5 Home Office report, 2000.

6 British Medical Association GP Committee chairman, 27 December 2001.

Dr Wendy Hirsh is an independent researcher and consultant in the fields of employee and management development, and strategic human resource planning. She works with many leading employers, in both the private and the public sectors, to examine their changing needs for people and how they might best be met. Wendy has a long-standing interest in career development from both the corporate and individual points of view, and in the relationship between these different perspectives.

6 | Careers in organisations – time to get positive

Wendy Hirsh

The whole idea of 'career development' at organisational level has got into a muddle. Most employees can't tell you the real mechanisms by which their organisations develop people's careers. Statements of employment strategy or policy now rarely include the word 'career', and talk in vague terms about 'developing yourself within the needs of the business'. Not surprisingly, employees give career development very low satisfaction-ratings in staff surveys. Managers feel uneasy about what they are supposed to be doing about their subordinates' careers. Organisations are not developing the careers and skills of their own employees dynamically enough to keep pace with changing business needs, and often can't recruit the people they need externally.

Major employers have got themselves into this muddle through a series of knee-jerk reactions to the real and significant changes in the career context, both within the organisation and outside it. The personnel profession and consultancy providers have made it worse by trying to invent 'products' or 'interventions' to make people feel as though something is being done about career development, but without addressing the underlying issues.

Starting from this somewhat dismal view, we shall try to paint a much more positive scenario of how businesses might handle career development. The elements of this more positive approach are already evolving in some large employing organisations that are rethinking what career development will really be about over the coming years, and how it can be supported.

Such rethinking demands we take a fresh look at:

- ◘ what we mean by 'career'

- ◘ why careers matter to both individuals and organisations

- ◘ how career development really takes place, and who does it.

The nature of the muddle
The myth of the past

The accepted story of the decline of the corporate career often starts with a Golden Age in which

> *'The "good old days" were actually not all that good … So let's not get carried away'*

large organisations managed people's careers effectively and employees rose merrily and at regular intervals through organisational hierarchies. The 'good old days' when organisations 'placed' people in jobs were actually not all that good. Processes were closed and careers often restricted by social class, educational background, old-boy networks, and narrow functional silos. So let's not get carried away by the Golden Age myth.

The negative nineties

Then along came the organisational upheavals of the 1980s and especially the 1990s. Much of what was said and written in the 1990s about careers in organisations concentrated on what organisations *couldn't* offer or *couldn't* do about careers. It was a response to uncomfortable changes that were taking place, especially those leading to redundancies and restructurings.

If we caricature these responses just a little, we can see just how ill-considered they were:

- ◘ We can't offer you a career for life – so we can't offer most staff 'careers' at all.

- ◘ Our best people may decide at any time to go elsewhere – so let's keep quiet about their career options and hope they stick with us.

- ◘ We don't know exactly what the future will hold – so let's focus all our discussions with employees on their current job roles.

- ◘ With flatter structures there may be less promotion – so we won't talk about career 'progression' in case we raise 'expectations'.

- ◘ We don't have detailed future career paths we can map out for people – so we can't tell them anything about how they might progress into more senior roles or move sideways from one kind of work into another.

- ◘ We do know that skills are important – so we'll talk about skills, competencies and learning instead of careers and work experiences.

- ◘ We can no longer manage people's careers for them – so we'll tell them that they now have to manage for themselves.

Bits of process

The cracks of this fundamentally negative view of careers have been thinly papered over by some HR processes – some fairly useful, others less so.

- ◘ Succession planning is often introduced with the intention of managing careers more proactively for the 'high-potential' few. These small populations are also awarded other career goodies like development centres and mentors.

- ◘ Personal development plan (PDP) forms are included in appraisal documentation.

◘ Internal job vacancies are increasingly advertised to employees, and the line manager with the vacancy chooses between those who apply.

◘ Bosses are told that supporting the career development of subordinates is part of their job.

◘ HR people, meanwhile, are being 'strategic', and don't do anything as mundane as talking to employees about their careers.

Although this is a grossly over-simplified summary of what large organisations have been up to over the past 10 years, it's really not so far from the truth. There is some good practice in career development, especially for those 'special' groups who get individual attention. For the majority of employees, however, nothing purposeful really happens in respect of their careers. They have no serious discussion of their future options and do not know which of the jobs they see advertised internally they might sensibly apply for. Recent research shows that only a tiny proportion of useful career discussions take place in appraisal, and only a minority with the immediate boss.[1]

The future – facing the real career issues

So what scenarios can we see for the future?

Some organisations are going back to basics, re-thinking the meaning of careers and the way they might address the real career issues faced by their

people and their businesses. Let's look at what this involves – in my view, three major considerations.

Step 1 – remember why careers matter

One way to start is by remembering why 'careers' became important, and what they might mean in future.

Why *do* people still talk about their careers?

Even though organisations have tried to dis-invent 'careers', the use of the word and the ideas behind it have not gone away from ordinary conversation. Tube-trains are full of ads for universities and employment agencies offering better 'careers'. The word 'career' conveys something dynamic, future-looking, a sense of opportunity, something attractive – more than 'just a job'. When we want to understand the full significance of a working life we also use the term 'career'. The career of a Judi Dench is neither organisational nor hierarchical, but does convey the sum total of a body of work, a growth in skill, a progression and links between one work experience and another. Even criminals have careers.

Many of these ideas also surface if you ask employees in large organisations what they mean by the word 'career'. A recent study did just this with over 100 junior and middle managers in large organisations.[2] Their replies were rich and varied, and included the following meanings of the word 'career':

- a journey and sense of direction – 'Career has been the road I wanted to go along, the things I wanted to do.'

- change, challenge, interest, and personal growth – 'Career is about enjoying what I do, something to have a stab at.'

- impact and contribution – 'I want to build on the past and have more impact.'

- self-preservation and employability – 'Positioning yourself to work within the goals that the company has – sniffing the wind.'

- skills and CV – 'My skill-set is my base. I am accumulating experience, getting more money, making myself more marketable. I see this as a continuous evolution.'

Interestingly, this same sample was asked what they thought the term 'development' meant. They saw it as a word invented by HR people to be a new jargon term for training. They did not know whether it had any relevance to their career issues or in what way 'personal development' might be relevant to them.

> **'Keeping employees at a standstill where they are, in skill and job terms, is not a realistic option.'**

Why should organisations bother with careers? It is equally important to remember that organisations still need employees to have 'careers'.

Organisational careers became important because large employers have always needed to grow the higher-level or company-specific skills that they could not easily recruit. Those skills must also be deployed effectively across the organisation. The development and deployment of shifting skill-sets over time is what career development means to the organisation. It is an even more pressing challenge today. With fewer people and more work to do, organisations have to achieve both high job performance and active career development for most of their employees. Keeping employees at a standstill where they are, in skill and job terms, is not a realistic option.

Step 2 – transmit a realistic but positive message for the future

So the negative messages of the 1990s have not positioned us well for the future. A more positive career message is needed. We must face up to the real uncertainties of organisational life, but also acknowledge that active career development is required by the business as well as by the individual:

- We can't offer you a career for life – but we want you to progress your career for as long as you stay with us.

- Our best people may decide at any time to go elsewhere – so we shall get to know them very well and try to make the best possible use of their abilities. We know this is our best bet for keeping them.

◘ We don't know exactly what the future will hold – so we shall make sure that our employees understand as much as they can about the business and the changing labour market, so that they can have several realistic future options in mind.

◘ With flatter structures there may be less promotion – so we are realistic about the likely amount of upward job movement and make sideways moves genuinely accessible.

◘ We don't have detailed career paths we can map out for people – so we paint broader pictures of the types of work we have, and of how people can move within and between them.

◘ We do know that skills are important – so we help employees to understand the relationships between the jobs we have and the skills needed to do those jobs.

◘ We can no longer manage people's careers for them – so we shall work with our employees as active partners in their careers. We shall seek to increase the contribution they can make to the business over time, taking account of their aspirations and preferences.

Some organisations are already espousing this more positive model, although they still often lack the nerve to take a deep breath and use the 'c–' word in a positive way.

It can seem easier to couch a more positive stance on career development in terms of a 'service' to employees – almost as part of the benefits package or as a 'soft and fluffy' part of the employment relationship. Bearing in mind the importance of careers to the business as well as to employees, we need to knock the 'soft and fluffy' thing hard on the head.

Career development is important to individuals *and* to businesses, and the trick is to aim for 'win-win' outcomes at the individual level. As Peter Herriot has explained[3], this implies a career 'partnership' in which information is exchanged and negotiations take place between the organisation and the employee over possible job moves and investment in learning.

Step 3 – deliver on the core aspects of career development

The real test of this more positive pudding, of course, will be in the eating. So what practical changes in the way we deal with careers are needed to make this more positive scenario come to life? What would it *look like* for an organisation to be a more positive partner with its employees in their career development? How can 'win-win' outcomes be reached? Who should do what?

One way forward in this is to stop thinking about lists of possible interventions (mentors, development centres, counselling services, etc) and start with a list of core deliverables, which can then be achieved in many different ways, depending on the types of employee, the size and the management culture of the organisation. These deliverables should include:

◘ feedback for individuals on their skills and performance, but also on how the organisation sees their potential and how they 'stack up' – appraisal can be good for giving performance feedback, but it is a weak vehicle for assessing potential. Employees get better feedback for career purposes by talking more informally to various people who can shed light on how they appear to others. Organisations are better placed to give feedback on potential if there is some collective process by which a number of managers discuss an individual and reach a shared view. This is a key part of good succession planning, but is usually carried out in respect of only limited populations. The 'development cell' process at Rolls-Royce is an example of how groups of managers can come together to discuss the career development of individuals who work in their function or unit. They reach a more considered view than the line manager can easily achieve alone. Such discussions cover substantial populations of employees. They feed back to the employee information on how the company sees his or her potential, possible career direction and development needs. It is then up to the individual to take the lead in acting on this information.

◘ information on current and future jobs and career options – This is vital to employees when thinking about their careers. Senior managers often have a much broader view of such matters than more immediate bosses. HR people also have valuable tacit information about the organisation and can help employees network across divisions, functions and locations to find out what they need to know. Some organisations are putting useful career information on their intranets. Nestlé, for example, provides the names of contacts in a range of jobs willing to talk to any employee about the kind of work they do.

◘ advice – This plays a crucial part in good career decisions. Useful advice can be strategic (on a major career change) or tactical (on whether to accept a project opportunity or apply for a particular job). The best advice is often informal and from people whose judgement and discretion can be trusted. Some employees occasionally need more in-depth help – closer to what we might call career counselling. It can be useful to have this more specialised service available from well-trained individuals in HR, often as part of a wider employee development role.

◘ career education – This may be something we associate with school, but many adults need it too. People often lack simple ways of thinking about careers and the practical skills to find out about jobs, make a good job application, elicit support from others, and so on. Some information can be imparted through workbooks. Such career planning tools are now moving on to interactive computer packages in organisations such as Nationwide and Lloyds TSB. Formal or informal mentors also provide career education. Some companies, including Sun Microsystems, have used career workshops to give employees an injection of career skills which they can hopefully draw on for many years. Core management training should equip managers to support other people's careers. BP has just included this in their new worldwide programme for first-line managers.

- access to learning – This is often thought of as a 'training' process, not a 'career' process, but the two are inextricably linked. People who are good at managing their careers take full advantage of formal training and are very aware of learning from every job experience they have, including projects and assignments. However, many employees feel at present that training investment is too limited to the jobs they are doing today and not sufficiently directed at preparing them for the future

- access to progressive job experiences – Now this is the heart of career development. There is not much point doing lots of personal planning, training and soul-searching if the organisation blocks you from moving to a job in which you can develop further and increase your contribution or satisfaction. Open internal job markets are a great help – but only on two conditions. First, employees need advice on how to select realistic job moves. Second, the internal appointment process must temper the idea of 'best fit' selection with the notion of a developmental element in appointments. In other words, every new job should afford you some new learning as well as using your existing skills – performance plus career development. Competence-based selection methods can squeeze out career development if they are implemented narrowly. Employees can find themselves in a Catch-22 situation in which they are told to develop their own skills and careers by applying for internal vacancies, but can't get appointed to jobs that require skills they don't already have.

> *'The end-point should be to weave the idea of "career" back into normal working life from whence it arose.'*

In this positive career future, more organisations will support these core elements of career development for all employees who have the inclination and ability to adopt a positive attitude to their own working lives. They will do so because of the gain to their businesses of really taking the lid off what their people can achieve. As we have illustrated, there is immense latitude in how such career support can be given. It is important to recognise, however, that informal career support based on relationships is likely to be more important than formal career 'processes' designed by the HR function. The end-point should be to weave the idea of 'career' back into normal working life from whence it arose. Career development should be a mainstream activity for employees, not some mysterious 'service' delivered by specialists, or an optional extra for the favoured few.

References

1 Hirsh W., Jackson C. and Kidd J. M. (2001), *Straight Talking: Effective career discussions at work*, Cambridge, NICEC/CRAC.

2 'Spinal accord', *People Management*, 25 May 2000.

3 Herriot P. and Pemberton C. (1995), *New Deals*, Chichester, John Wiley.